Fishers of Men

For
Diane
love, Kisses, dreams
forever
Thank You,
Kath Orr

Fishers of Men

poems by

KATE GALE

Red Hen Press   *Los Angeles 2000*

Fishers of Men

Grateful acknowledgment is made to the editors of the following journals in which these poems first appeared:

Caprice: "Prozac"
Chatahooche Review: "Twilight in Peru"
The Chester H. Jones Foundation Anthology: "What I Did Not Tell Anyone"
Eclipse: "The Way I Learned to Write," "Walking off into the Night Sky,"
     "The Advice I Missed," and "The Word No"
Mudfish: "Fish Ball Soup"

Photo & cover image by Mark E. Cull
Book and cover design by Mark E. Cull

First Edition
ISBN 1-888996-27-7
Library of Congress Catalog Card Number: 00-103833

Published by

Red Hen Press
www.redhen.org

for Nicholas

Table of Contents

I   *Blue*

The Last Photograph	13
The Hand on the Doorknob	14
Ammunition and Cows	16
Lilac Time	18
Prayer over Green Onions	20
The Painted Worshipper	22
Prozac	23
The Pool I Never Had	24
Fish Ball Soup	28
The Word "No"	30
An Easy Way Toward Sleep	32
No One Has Gone Down on Me in Weeks	34
The Advice I Missed	36
What I Did Not Tell Anyone	38
Walking off into the Night Sky	39
Joy of Sex	40

II   *Gray*

Everyone Has a House	45
Mostly White	46
Romeo and Juliet Survive	47
Urban Gorillas	48
Garlic and Mushrooms	50
Heat Swims in My Eyes	52
Half Civilized, Half Naked	54
Staying with Corduroy	56
Calling Down Rain	57
Mustard, Onion, Pickle	58
Tiger's Cry	60
Yucatán Goodbyes	62
Glass Air	64

Twilight in Peru   66
Ad Infinitum   68
Beards as Weapons   70

III   *Red*

Our Bedclothes   73
Fishers of Men   74
Reasons to Undress a Woman Quickly   76
Cities   78
Trains   80
Trapping Rats and Other Problems   81
Giraffe Tongues and Cherries   82
The Dream You Couldn't Leap Across   84
What is Left   86
Next to the Freeways   88
Missing the Crow   90
Not Needing the Sun   92
She Told Me She Would Cure Him of Hitting Her   94
Rinsing Cherries   95
You Never Married the Pope   96
There's Nothing to Talk About in this Poem   98

IV   *Green*

Praying Mantises and Missiles   101
I Give You My Hand   102
The Way I Learned to Write   104
Witchy Hands   106
Inventing Royalty in Bed   107
You Do Frighten Me   108
The Edges of Elbow Sleep   110
Undressing Kathy   112

Holiness is . . .   114
Marsupial Love   115
Wooden Salt Shaker   116
Tuesdays   118
Reasons Why He Hurt You   120
Breakfast   121
Bed Vision   122
Across the Street   124
The Emperor's New Clothes   126
Tundra Races   127

I
Blue

The Last Photograph

In the small photograph,
my mother has her eyes closed.
I am shapeless, rather pale
probably two. There is snow.
My sister has a sled.
It is only a year before
my mother will abandon me
to be beaten, brainwashed.
For years I was sure that
she despised that shapeless creature
until I looked carefully
and realized I'd been buried in snow
up to the armpits.
She was sitting there, eyes closed
that thing that had been her daughter
already a part of the landscape,
her mind already gone.

The Hand on the Doorknob

A white room, bare wood floor, a sleeping bag, no chair
a shelf with two books, one a Bible. The room faces west.
It is full of shadows. Trees cover one window.
The sun sets in the other, the panes hold the sun's face.
A girl shut up alone ten days, not a good girl.
She eats her one bowl of cold oatmeal, slowly,
licks the bowl carefully, drinks water from a jug
pees in another, tries to keep the two jugs even.
This is entertainment. Reads the book
that is not the Bible, practices holding her breath.
Her one bathroom break is across the hall.
The bathroom impossibly bright, the sound of a vacuum,
gleaming tiles, sensory overload.
Back in the room, the Bible. She reads every story on lepers,
their bodies decaying, turning white, pieces falling off.
Ten days; the door knob turns.
Her mother leads her down stairs across the courtyard
where the stars are, plants, the smell of cows.
Assembly time, eighty children watch her walk
to the front of the room. The light bulbs bare florescent,
her face sick yellow, she tastes bile.
The girl rode bareback at night after the lights were out,
got caught. She walks straight to the center of the room
dull metal, ropes, thin wrists, heavy stick,
blow after blow, the girl thinks of nothing,
screams once, then feels a thudding in her brain.
They tell her later, the beating went on
as her head sagged between her arms,
but she only remembers the first blow, the second,
and then black and she's dreaming of horseback riding
at midnight through the room with white walls.
Then cold water, voices, pain, grownup voices, pain.
Shut that out, dream again. Practice now.
Grownup voices, pain. Dream.
Ice water pouring down now.

The white room is round; it is a womb shell.
Say I'm home. If you meet someone who sees through it,
says, hey, this is opaque; it's a membrane.
Hey, I see you in there! Don't respond.
If they say, I see you in there
I love you in there,
Run, dragging your shell. It's all you have.

Without that, who are you really?
You don't.
You don't want to find out?
Do you?

Ammunition and Cows

A boy I called my friend
showed me his hands
in the light of our flashlights
and began to tell me
their stories

How he'd knelt behind a cow
in serious contemplation of her udder
taken it to his mouth
one teat at a time
to drink calf-like

How the cow went on chewing
and he felt his first erection
reached for himself let more milk flow
I was amazed at what became "himself"
in the story

His real self lurking
there in his trousers
and the story tangled with
my view that men were moss-covered stones
green and soft looking, hard underneath

He asked me to think of his hand
curved around himself, take pity on him
do something about this problem
at fourteen what could I imagine doing
the image of the cow held me but I had no milk

The mammal in me longed to show him
where hair grew
take his head down to lie between my breasts
tell him why women are better than cows
and I was pretty sure of this

but I wasn't sure about "himself"
the image left me reeling breathless
I wondered about men in barracks
with their rifles and themselves
all that ammunition crowded close

His hands were small schoolboy hands
not yet dangerous, later
he would join the army go overseas
shoot to kill but that day
he begged me to on his knees
his head leaning on my thighs

When I reach for myself he said
I want it to be your hands
come let me show you
you'll see something you never imagined
let me see your hands

and that was all he asked really
to show me this version of himself
to lose control on a girl's belly
let me feel for milk he said
someday you'll have some

and in this too he was right

Lilac Time

> Go down to Kew in lilac-time, in lilac-time, in lilac-time;
> Go down to Kew in lilac-time (it isn't far from London!)
> And you shall wander hand in hand with love in summer's wonderland;
> Go down to Kew in lilac-time (it isn't far from London!)

—Alfred Noyes

When you gave me something purple
I fell asleep declaring lilacs not to be my flower
Too loud too early too heavy-scented
and above all unwilling to close up at night

My girlhood was spent in lilac time
my hands rushing with their scent
I swore I wouldn't bring them to my face
but my lovers begged

and the lilacs themselves
finally pulled me into their shadowy secret
lilacs blooming day and night
in the kitchen the lawn

but especially in the glade
behind my father's house
I would squat behind the poplars
eyes closed smelling enormous lilacs

praying for rain
Thick fog rain
lilac scented
mornings with petals in my teeth

When Mother found us there
she cried Bless me Father for I have sinned
He promised a wedding
in the fantastic chapel of peace

Mother's face was evening air
a vacant twilight of stillness
and I was hungry
for lilacs and hated them too

gorging with scent
faint with nausea at their bursting ripeness
heavy purple
I said yes to lilacs for a lifetime

never really wanting the novelty
of taking lilac into my clover
lilac cream on my fingers
I drown so in the scent and dream lilac dreams

It's everywhere
my father told me
smiling secretly when I first
discovered the glade at thirteen

and now
as my daughter sleeps
I watch her eyelashes carefully
for petalled dreams

Prayer over Green Onions

Since fall we've lived in a different apartment
than the one we were evicted from in April.
In between we stayed on a mattress
in our friend Meena's carport. It was nice.
The neighbor cats dropped off dead birds.
We got a fan to lift the carpet of heat.
Meena fried chicken.

This place since fall has jail bars
on the windows and a lot of noise
from who's being slapped around in our building.
Crazy people, somebody with garlic on their front door.
A woman comes out on her balcony every morning naked
holding a bunch of green onions
at her throat, prays facing east.

The prayer is useless,
but I understand the green onions.
Though I would hold some full ripe tomatoes
and a couple of ears of corn.
I would pray naked only if I had a good body
and a god who was into that.
My mother's god is into nuns.

I am ribs and shoulder blades.
I rustle through school taking notice of nothing
but getting back home without having my ribs crack.
Home is where I'm pretty safe now.
He doesn't come around much. With the TV
and peanut butter I can be happy even when.
Until we gotta move again.

Nobody really interests me.
There's nothing I think about, nowhere I'm going.
I'm not going to be anything
but another set of eyes
staring down a long fire escape
noticing the last twenty steps are missing
and it's too far to jump.

I'll be under city sky, my skin
dark and shining and unnoticed,
green onions in hand
letting go of prayers
that sink, shudder,
go down through sewers
through the long drain and out to sea.

The Painted Worshipper

Lily prays for the sick, the dying, those that are lost,
arranges her strapless sundress
under its becoming violet jacket.
She wonders if Charlie will ask her to lunch.

The dog laps the man's hands, a frantic washing.
The dog's body wriggles. He leaps, he begs, he rolls
in a whirl of admiration for the young man
with the ball, the bones at night from plastic bags.

His wife makes his favorite dinner, baked salmon
roast potatoes, Chardonnay, a light cake.
She chatters about shoes. She is very attentive.
Her birthday is coming.

Prozac

He said
if I have a very limited time
on this planet,
and I believe I do,
let me spend it
taking Prozac.
Prozac because I don't have
to deal with any
bad feelings
and I like that.
Like let's say
my tire goes flat
or my roof is leaking
I just say, Ah well.

And I say,
what about fighting in Indonesia
or killings in Afghanistan?
and he says,
Prozac takes care of that too.
I'm too happy to let it bother me.
I'd like the children
to take it he says.
There's a great future for our family.
And we'll look so American in pictures.
Except for me, I say
I'll always be moody
and there to spoil things.

The Pool I Never Had

Along the ridge of the house
where we used to live
a row of pine trees
one could see over
to the mountains beyond.

The trees were dwarfed
grappling with their roots
on a sandy hillside
overlooking a ravine.
The children climbed down
that ravine.

You remember?
onc January day trying to escape,
the fights we got into those days
the children came up bubbly
with poison oak, festering, oozing
like children of the plague.

All last night while it rained,
the sky a blister trying to break
onto the already sodden earth.
I remember how
we ended it then.

I loaded those children
who could barely see from their eyes
and were trying to hear nothing
into my car, left the house
but especially the pool

which you would never finish.
When we bought the house,
I had wanted a pool
so we had one dug, cemented,
but you said pools were dangerous

no more money,
the pool had eaten your savings.
I pictured the pool like a bear
tearing into your bank account
a huge fish.

The concrete pit
collected water, mosquitoes.
It became rank for two summers
the fence rusting
the pool equipment

a convenient roost
for the chickens.
I used the fenced pool for our poultry.
Ducks swam in the fetid water
You used to drink Coors in a deck chair,

watch the ducks.
You'd get a tan while the ducks
got down in all that green slime,
so last night in the rain,
I'd been wondering about you all week

and whether I'd done the right thing,
I drove out to that house,
all that rain closing in on me
threatening to lift my car
threatening to carry me away.

I approached the house
from the street below.
Looking up, saw something
coming. I drove backward
because sometime you do have to back up.

Because it was coming,
what I saw first was that row of trees
branches crashing
down the ravine sloping down in a mass
of showered branches and after them

the pool,
like a concrete boat
wrenched off its mooring.
It came, tipping down the slope
like an ocean liner

picking up speed as it slid
over tree branches to the river
flowing under the street, and I
saw it shoot out the other side
rumbling between the banks of the wash

the concrete sides chewing up dirt.
Inside I could still hear the ducks
quacking, protesting.
I did not look for your house
I did not rescue those ducks.

The life I saved was my own,
and my children's.
Enough lives for one person.
The pool was going its own way
The pool had never been mine,
had never been ours.

Fish Ball Soup

Nobody can say
this is not good soup
the noodles thick and wide
the cilantro green and spring
in the bowl

In the beginning
I called him "Presh"
When he showed me San Francisco
I felt him pulling me across
the Golden Gate into his country

The soup strangely filling
for all its clear liquid
the waiter gives me a white spoon
green onions fish balls
Hong Kong it says on the wall

My husband pulled my head
back by my hair
said Aren't you a nice one?
Wake up!
Get on your knees!

The soup has a strange flavor
nothing I grew up with
there's lime under the broth
I'm sure if you add milk
it will curdle and stink

a thin line of blood
See this knife?
he laughs
okay you don't like that?
okay

But I do like the soup
I eat it
stopping and starting
The music rises
crackles of Chinese opera

I still take his hand odd moments
count on him to fix the sink
tell me when I'm getting fat
follow me around the house pointing
to what needs done

The soup gets cold
I can't finish it
I'm going to walk away
leave it here   .
To hell with soup

You got a traffic ticket?
You did what?
Next time get down on your knees girl.
Suck that cop off!
Suck him off!

The soup bowl clatters
to the ceramic tile floor
I don't even apologize
Just slap down my money
on the way out.

The Word "No"

Essays have been written on men
not understanding the word "no,"
not accepting it,
trying to change a no to a yes,
a one syllable word
evolving so the race can go on.

I think about women and no.
No is not really
in the vocabulary for me.
If I stretch out
toward my partner
the answer is always, When?

For me,
the answer has always been yes,
now, let's go
to dinner
on a date, to lunch
to bed.

When I hear no,
I think of it as a yes
in a different form
a yes in the making
a yes that requires female attention,
the right underwear.

I wonder about men
and how they handle no
how horrible it would be
to sit there ready, erect
and have no
put in your lap.

We give you no
because we make 70 cents
on the dollar
no because of childbirth
no because
it is something we can do.

An Easy Way Toward Sleep

At first it was funny.
She would wake him in the night,
pry him out of sleep,
ask, do you really love me?
They fell in love on vacation.
Then they went back to work.

She woke him, her hands raking the air
Do you love me?
Midnight, three in the morning.
Yes, he'd say watching her like a shadow puppet
the hall light on her ferocious bedroom hair.
Can I go back to sleep now?

Sometimes she'd get fruit,
a bowl of cherries or some papayas,
sit cross legged on the bed.
Are you sure? Can we talk about it?
It wasn't that she got up two hours later than he.
She would have waked him regardless.

She was like a cat stalking him.
Do you want that redhead? she'd ask,
as they passed some glistening hard body on the beach.
Like he could say, no, the very thought
of that woman bouncing in the sunlight
makes me physically ill.

When he said, I need sleep, she brooded.
When he said, I love you, she pondered.
When he said, believe me, she winced
and stared for hours at her father's photograph.
All right, he said, all right.
He made love to her every night.

He allowed no breathing space.
She began to see colors.
He let her cry for mercy.
She began to need sleep badly.
It was easier than talking about it.
It was easier than words.

No One Has Gone Down on Me in Weeks

Anxiety attacks in the night
I'm drunk
or was when I fell asleep
still may be for all I know
which isn't much
You were poking at me
or you were doing something
interesting with your hands
can't remember
My intestines ache
so I turn on the blue
hotel tv light
why is it always blue?

What's going on in America?
I'm glad to know
because my liver is poisoned
my breath a sour mess
sunlight smells of sewer
and wet dogs
The night shifts around me
hot wind from the open window
punctuated by blasts
from the air conditioner
I don't understand why
the little jets
coming from my lit cigarette
don't calm me anymore

The world is ending very fast
no one has gone down on me in weeks.
I flip through channels
so I know what I don't like
that's going on
that's causing me to get sick like this
I say to you
hold on shut up wake up
you're snoring
Do you have any idea?
but you are dead asleep
and will probably be speechless
in the morning

The Advice I Missed

You said
What's wrong
with cabbage and potatoes?
You said
What were you
expecting anyhow?
You said
Get out of here
with that look
like you're disgusted
with me or something
You said
come back here
You said
Where are you going?
You said
the food's on the table
the bread's half eaten
The children are unbathed
the laundry undone
You said
Get your head down
out of the rafters
You'll get dust
in your ears
I said
Isn't it clouds?
You said
You can't think that high
You said
I love you
but I'm sick of your behavior
You said
Behave yourself
and everything will be easier

You said
Don't screw up
I fell asleep
When I woke
you were talking
to the wall behind me
I had probably
missed the best advice
I cannot say
I was disappointed

What I Did Not Tell Anyone

That I loved nursing.
That I nursed each baby
Whether they were hungry or not.
That they were always hungry.
That milk flowed like tears.
That my blouses were always damp.
That one night, I lay on my side,
baby nursing from midnight
until 2 in the morning.
That he finally took me
while the child nursed.
That I felt my whole family
greedily feeding off me.
That my body felt stolen.
That I felt like Russia during all the wars
troops tramping over me on their way to Moscow.
That he didn't say anything
That the baby fell asleep.
That I wanted to sleep alone.
That the sky was still very dark.
That I left the house in my bathrobe.
That the streetlights begged me to go back.
That the streetlights said,
men and babies are waiting for you.
That the streetlights were traitors.

Walking off into the Night Sky

After the divorce flies spread all over the Valley
A chill night an open doorway
completely naked I smelled the air
sage and desert orange blossoms and horse dung
A person can wake in the wrong skin
do things inside their skin
that will leave them outside the house
the night cricketing and humming
I have very long hair but I didn't feel it
felt bald of my senses

My husband came outside to bring me a blanket
he turned something over and over in his hands
There was the blanket around me
there was my soon to be ex-husband
turning this thing over and over in his hands
and there were flies buzzing
The city of Los Angeles
is not a place for introspection
The palm trees etched against the sky
defied me to find anything wrong with the skyline

But I had weaned the baby
and was ready to walk.

Joy of Sex

One year after marriage
the *Joy of Sex*, a wedding gift
from a thoughtful friend
who said inspiration is the key
but education hones technique,
fell behind our water-bed
irretrievable.
Of course we tried
after that,
but things were not the same.

Thongs, garters, silk scarves,
high·heels, flash lights, toe rings,
glow-in-the-dark condoms
plastic noses, maple syrup,
masks with extra facial hair,
nipple rings, clothespins
orangutan photos,
that Rabbi mask you used to wear,
scared the hell out of me
nothing was quite the same.

I used to bite my nails
thinking about sex,
and then there were issues:
the kids, money, fights over your mother,
you wearing overalls at parties,
your brother throwing up on the lawn,
my best friend sleeping with your best friend,
the Lipton tea fight
where you said all I get is Lipton tea because
I don't love you.

Never considering that
I'm just not a very creative shopper.
Well, you thought it was my going off to grad school.
But me? As I told one therapist after another,
just before our marriage drew its final breath
off the rocky shores of northern Nova Scotia,
it was the damned book disappearing,
that's what started it all,
or ended it all,
one of those, I told them.

II
Gray

Everyone Has a House

What I like about your country
she tells me is the toilets
I wouldn't mind bringing one home
but it wouldn't do much good
she says she likes the bathtubs
and the refrigerators
but she is not so crazy
about the tortillas
which are not made properly
or the cilantro which tastes like soap
Also the freeways ruin the landscape
and the children watch television
when they could be playing soccer
and the teenagers stare at their parents
with bare faces that say
give it to me
and the abuelitos are like dogs
to the children
the children walk by with no respect
mangoes here are not so good
not enough rain
and the women here have so many clothes
I think your country has the most wonderful bathrooms
and everyone has a house
although tents would be nicer
I think or boats
or even just sleeping in a tree
My family has a tree
we live under
but the tree has no toilet
I grant you that.

Mostly White

What she doesn't understand,
the girl tells me,
is that I'm partly white.
I've got a lot of white in me
from my mother's side.
My sisters look white,
but me, I'm dark,
and she doesn't know that.
She pushes me around like I'm dumb.
It's like she doesn't even see me
when she looks at me.
It's like she's looking someplace else.
It's like I'm saying,
Treat me with some respect.
Don't I deserve that?
And she's seeing a piece of dirt
on the sidewalk, and she's telling me,
Missy, Missy, who do you think you are?
Who does she think she is?
to decide me and my kids don't get to eat?
The truth is, she doesn't know who she's dealing with.
I'm bringing in a picture next time
to show her. She'll see
my sisters in the picture.
She'll see them, 'cause right away
you can tell, they're mostly white.

Romeo and Juliet survive

Light enters pale gray and Juliet begins to retch.
Romeo strokes her hair; they make their way to the plaza.
It occurs to them that they are underage parents-to-be
with no jobs. Their families are still sharpening knives,
talking about collecting shotguns. Romeo suggests
they get out of town. Romeo wears a fur coat, Juliet a thin silk
dress. On the train they sit across from each other except
when Juliet is retching. At the next city, stone walls rise
around them and a group of prisoners shamble by, legs
shackled together. One spits on Romeo. Romeo screams
obscenities. The prisoner manages to punch him, breaking
gentle Romeo's collarbone.

Romeo works as a desk clerk in a hotel for prostitutes,
Juliet a waitress. When the rent is two months late
Juliet gives a man his simple request for half the money and
Romeo gives a man a less-than-complicated gesture
of affection for the other half.
By the time the baby is born,
Juliet is a small town prostitute, Romeo a thief
They celebrate the birth by robbing their parents
of some jewelry they feel they are entitled to.
Their son can handle a gun in both hands
shoot a moving target by age five.

Stay in the family business
Romeo tells him
Juliet smiles and wonders
how many prostitutes
Romeo is pimping for.

Urban Gorillas

Unsanctified

Oh Calvin, in your jeans
barely held up with a belt,
oh Calvin, without a thought
the TV hasn't handed you.
Look, there she comes,
cheerleader thin,
cheerleader fuckable, wantable, suckable.
All you have to do is grin and she's yours.
You can be gorilla stupid,
it doesn't matter, stud, just smile.
You think she knows better?
The sky will open.
Her dress will float up like a kite.
You're the stand-up comedian of her dreams.
You make her as happy as Sunday-morning cartoons.
Her laughter floats out and away
over passersby in lambskin coats
and gardeners with calloused palms.
Your Daddy's golf bag contains all the treasures
in the world. You're America.
You'll have your wife and lawn and fast foods
and snacks during Super Bowl Sunday
and beer and wisecracks and TV hum
and the yearly air show with those fighter planes,
make you proud,
make you glad to be a man
and peanuts at the ball game
and Jennifer the blueprint girl
with those perfect cheeks,
suck you off on those weeks
when the wife's out of town.
It's not really cheating.
It's the American way.
Buy condoms.
Buy American condoms

Be safe.
Wal-Mart is coming to your neighborhood.
Oh Calvin for chrissakes,
don't let the Commies get to you.
Don't let them tell you any different.
This is America, boy,
Fuck *them*.

Garlic and Mushrooms

Buses stop for everyone in Mexico.
Soon you have the whole world in your lap
a child sprawled across your knees
nursing from the mother beside you
across the aisle a man pulling your sleeve
offering to sell you fresh mangoes he sliced
with that machete leaning against you.
The restless flies form clouds of movement.
Someone gets on all Sunday-dressed
in a white embroidered shirt carrying a live chicken.
Everybody agrees it's a fine chicken, a good dinner.
There are suggestions as to how to cook it.
Somebody says roast with chili.
Others say a stew would be good.
But why stew it? it's young.
Stews are for old stringy birds;
this one's not stringy. Just perfect.
You agree; the chicken looks you in the eye.
But then the subject of mushrooms comes up
how good mushrooms and garlic are with chicken.
Perhaps even lime soup would hit the spot.
The heat is suffocating, sweat is all you taste.
Mushrooms are a good idea, you agree and cerveza.
Yes, that's generally agreed, cerveza with this chicken.
The hen herself seems indifferent to these arrangements
her bird eyes blinking in the hard light.
The bus driver keeps smoking and driving
fast as if rushing into the next world
were the purpose of this journey.
The air's suffused with heat; when the bus stops
it is for a cow and pig trying to cross the road.
The cow and pig do not hurry;
a man gets on rather dirty and rank smelling
like he's slept in a stable and washed in a river,
you squeeze closer to the nursing mother.

You blink back sweat, close your eyes
You are neither crouching, nor cringing.
You are neither angry nor dissatisfied
You have been moving in the direction of soup since
the first day of your life.

Heat Swims in My Eyes

The car fender sank beneath the weight
of the oncoming truck, and our journey
with its sand in the eyes collapsed.
I couldn't remember the shape of it
before the car crumpled our thoughts.
Heat swims in my eyes.
The woman across the street combing her hair.
The restaurant where we'd gone for dinner
had black beans, but no more singers.
They were washing the floor with a garden hose.
The cook blew her nose on the last of the napkins.
The man arrived for the car, eyes shining green.
The woman across the street
began to sing about the end of the world.
The man fixed the car before we had time
to clear our heads from last night's beer.
Back to Mérida the sun glaring.
In the airport he asks for all my money
to buy a beer, a car, a house, a picnic life.
I say no.
He says yes.
I say, no fair.
His boss says Pay.
I say, I don't think so.
He says now.
I say never.
He says all your money.
I call the police.
He winks at the police.
I say you devil.
The policeman reaches for a gun.
I say maybe.
All the police touch their guns.
I reach for my wallet.
They all smile.

They backslap and order beer
on my way out and scream,
"A las putas"
all over town
with my money.

Half Civilized, Half Naked

His niece, he thought,
was ready for anything,
so he jumped her
by the blue door
of her grandmother's
restaurant, which was
not really a restaurant
just a tiny fixed up taco stand
with a sign nobody
could make out.
The restaurant blew around
in the wind trying
to find a permanent location
for its boards and shingles.

He jumped her, pulled her
into the room where she
and her grandmother slept,
his nails scratching her skin
separating her from the cool safe air.
The girl's pink sweater
with which she wiped her nose
along the filthy sleeves lay crumpled.
She made almost no sounds,
a smothered cry once
in the tiny glow
that squeezed between the sheets
hanging over the window
and the wall she stared into.

Years later, Lucia
lived in the room behind the taco stand
she'd built into a fine restaurant
with tables and chairs.
She lived with the woman with snake eyes
several large dogs and a few pigeons.
People would murmur into their hands
remembering her breasts
swelling into the summer
of her fourteenth year
her blouses very wet.
They talked about waste
until she called them
uncivilized and stupid.

The shape of her buttocks barely concealed
under blue fabric, the full red lips,
all for the woman with snake eyes.
And someone had seen them
half naked by the well
so who was calling who
uncivilized?
Lucia sold goat milk and cheese,
her fruit was well watered
and always tasty.
But the villagers suspected
that the men who came to the restaurant
in their white shirts and Sunday hats
got only second best,

that the best was kept for women
who came in alone, searching
for some piece of their life
that got left somewhere
or was never located
to begin with.

Staying with Corduroy

When she is left alone with her son's body,
she peels down the bloody corduroys, bathes
his legs because it will be the last time,
washes his hair, the nape of his neck. Silver
falls out of his shirt pocket. His face is round,
splattered with red dew drops, fingers still curved.

She takes his hand to her mouth,
rocks gently, singing to him.
If he isn't hungry any more, he won't come home
to eat. She had given him yellow socks for Christmas.
She pulls them off his feet. His toes
are perfectly lined up, his body unnaturally curved.

In the next room, someone is playing a waltz.
Sunlight rains down outside. A lot of people
are going to the beach, the radio says.
When she opens the door and sees someone
sleeping on the steps, the heat and light swirling
through the legs of the palm trees seem unbearable.

She steps back to the room with bloody corduroy
and the boy's face, lifts the shirt
ready now to see the truth that separates
one day from the next. She wants
the moment of her hand
where the heart should be to last.

The street can wait.
She will stay
with this boy's body
in the neck of night,
will never go through
to the open womb of a new day.

Calling Down Rain

Something dangerous about the smell of her eyes
and the tattoos on one bare arm as she leans against
the sill with its potted geranium and shouts down
to the kids below that this isn't their day
And when they ask why not sneering up at her
leather-cool
skateboard-cool
y'all-go-fuck-yourselves-cool
she says it's going to rain any minute now
Ain't you looked at the sky
and they look up
It's right blue California cloudless
and the one in leather says
Y'all going to make it rain witch?
and she holds up a long blade
of grass in the sunlight and spits on it
Just watch me she says
and they shred off screaming down the hill
But she's at it again whistling with the grass
one eye cocked to the sky until the clouds roll in
and the heat gets swallowed
as the tree buds swell with rain
I'll be damned, she says to the sky
if my children can't grow here.

Mustard, Onion, Pickle

She feels beautiful in her bones
liquid rising off her skin
the day she rides in the parade wearing red
the sun showering light on her
all the boys' faces
hers like gold in her pockets
She can choose the one with the whitest horses
one whose life curves toward success like a chariot
rippling Apollo across the skies over Pacoima

She is the beauty queen of the whole East Valley
Her brothers' grim faces ride beside her
their eyes sharpening knives ready weapons
She marries Omar who goes to church every year
moves her out to the white neighborhood stucco houses
she floats in behind the U-Haul unloading
potted peppers and statues
She learns from Sue how to make sandwiches
with corned beef mustard onion pickle

The night the neighborhood white men shoot Omar
by accident thinking he is a prowler
watering his own lawn at dusk
the beauty queen of Pacoima is learning
to line dance in a country western bar
The next few years will be spent wearing black
becoming the neighborhood specter
She will not move but will remain like Jesus
fixed to the cross in the iglesia

The men don't watch her walk by with her
corned beef mustard pickles onions rye bread
She is oval pawed round bear-like
She carries with her a fascination like leprosy
She is poisonous as toadstools
as unassailable for comments as a barrio
Her English is forgotten
Her hair cut short gleams like wet fur
her dreams parcel wrapped and invisible

The weight of gender rests lightly
on her thick shoulders
The palm trees are foreigners
It is she who belongs to the landscape
She sits on a stump in the yard
where her husband fell
If she understands English she makes no sign
If she remembers tortillas
she does not remember salsa.

Tiger's Cry

The house is protected by plywood
so nothing will happen there.
Except flies, lizards, worms,
blood from dead mosquitoes,
ants, spiders.
Fans slice through huge moths,
feathers even and then the sound of feet,
and the maids are at it again,
hurrying toward blood.

The man who walks past faces like walls,
dreams of something twisting,
wears boots to crush little things,
waves his hands for food to come.
The man does not believe Shosha
when she says the house is in danger.
The man waves his hands for Shosha
and danger to forever disappear
as the gods of heat vanish in twilight.

But he does move after another drink,
to the verandah
to touch the plywood.
Outside nobody.
The air flinching from the disturbance
caused by movement suddenly
on the far side of the clearing.
A head first.
Gray and impossibly large.

He has time for many thoughts
as rage pours through the elephant.
Each thought clipped by the next.
Never listen to people under you. His motto.
The idea of his own gravestone.
How big elephants are,
moths struggling for seconds
under nets that tangle thin soft wings
lifting the powdery dust
so they'll never fly again.

Ant stain on the walls,
the long cry of a tiger
unable to feed her young.
Thoughts pile
over each other headlong.
The plywood splinters,
and for a long second,
he hears the elephant's breath,
remembers a thousand faces.

The elephant did not sleep
at all well,
her brain a tornado
of loose thoughts
and the flies make her crazy.
Her feet move through something twisting.
She stamps out her own dreams
in a mass of splinters.
Somewhere, she hears a tiger's cry.

Yucatán Goodbyes

She squats in a house with a straw roof
to feed her husband soup
a piece of turkey.
It is their secret
the soup, the dirt floor
the shedding of life.
There is a hospital in a city
blindingly hot and far away.
He says he will be buried soon enough.
Why leave the shade
of the thatched roof
sooner than necessary?
The wood sticks present combed light
across the hammock
where he rocks.
The woman picks up her sewing,
sings to him.
He catches her voice threads,
readies himself.
It has all been very much as she expected.
She has carried seventeen children
seven who lived,
has used her fingers
to cut and sew.
Her husband has built a house,
a thatched roof
danced with her in the plaza.
The children
he fathered in other pueblos
have come to pay their respects to her.
She has combed their hair
over eyes like his
made them lime soup.
The heat has softened her movements
until they are rounded.

She sings now.
A turkey vulture flaps
over the hut, lands.
We're not ready, she says to the bird
I'm not finished with this song.

Glass Air

There was that suspended moment
glass air
Her skin liquid
warm amber
not translucent
the way skin is in movies
This skin
spread out over the body
warm and radiant
as a field of poppies

Then his moustache
touching her face saying
It is dangerous
to leave one country
for another
He drinks a beer
eats watching her
He is hungry
She knows this
and is afraid

He reaches into empty pockets
Her pockets are all sewn
inside jackets
He moves to help her into
the jacket
Below them at the fountain
a young girl leans over
to press her fingers into the water
exposing the hollow of her throat
the dip of her breasts

The woman in the jacket
feels exposed
turns away
I have this to worry about
she says
She reaches her arms out
into the raw air
and the rain begins
soft at first
then cold

Always? she asks the man
his moustache wet
from leaning out
Always he says
the rain
a fact of life

Twilight in Peru

for Lori Berenson

You cannot understand twilight
as we understand it.
We have stood in the curtain
of mountain air in Peru, outside a prison
that holds our daughter.
We have held the twilight air
very softly, like holding round balls
in vast shimmering hallways.
All around us, noises
animal twilight.
Knowing that where our daughter is,
it is already dark,
That she feels slowly
along the walls of her cell
for the door.

How she got here
is a story
too long
for us to tell.
She was an observer,
one of the note-takers
of the world.
But she forgot,
or we forgot to tell her,
to only take notes
of the oppressed preying
on each other
as we do at times.
To stop writing
when the oppressor appears.

To do anything else
to bake bread
to lie down
to stand up
to stand up naked
to lean against a tree
to smoke a cigarette
to smoke anything
to drink a beer
to see nothing
to be nothing
to be part of the relaxed
unconcerned
and soon-to-be-cut-down foliage
of another landscape

where the blood flows down
into the cracks of earth
while a thousand shining faces
peer from between bars
to watch the last of it disappear
in the fading ghastly twilight.

Ad Infinitum

Sheila broke a dinner plate
across young Tommy's face
during, after, or before breakfast.
Why quibble with details, your Honor?
These things happen all the time.

Poverty has its own rules,
punishments and diseases.
Don't screw with it. We are sand worms.
Everything on top is crystal chandeliers
hanging from an invisible sky dome.

Your Honor, your Holiness,
I never wanted a child,
this one or any of the others.
Nobody died, nobody suffocated, nobody drowned.
Nobody got sick worse than the measles.

Take a pill.
Take a friendly bit of advice.
Take some friendly medication
from your friendly neighborhood doctor.
There *is* a doctor in your neighborhood.

What I trained my kids to do is what you wanted.
Get up in the morning. Ignore the sky.
Watch television. Put on clothes.
Go to institution. Do institutional duty
pausing for institutional food.

Go home.
Turn on the television.
Eat.
Go to bed.
Insert or allow insertion

depending on your gender,
and sexual preference.
Sleep.
Repeat.
Ad infinitum.
Ad nauseam.
Someone hits the kid
to break the monotony.
Nobody gets hurt.

If anybody breaks a jaw,
Oh well.
Nobody gets fucked up.
Shut up.
I'm not thinking
about whatever it is you're saying.
Shut up.
Shut the fuck up.
Will you?
Can't you see
I'm watching fucking television?
Fuck you.

Beards as Weapons

for Karen

When my lover turned over the ten peso note
with Emiliano Zapata staring up at me
under the Mexican sky, I told him in Spanish
how I loved the beard he'd grown for me.
What I wanted with the beard on his face
is nobody's business, but that face
with its luxurious growth would come
between my North America and my South America
like the jungled neck of land
we so carelessly refer to as Central America.

His brain festered with platoons of logic.
Some afternoons I would just as soon sleep;
all he got from his rapid artillery fire
of discussion was static on my end.
Sometimes we tossed bowling pins back and forth
practicing the ancient form of juggling with new tools.
But with each new day, the landscape
with its intolerable light
and the webbed air of Spanish voices
turned love sour in the sunlight.

The day before we boarded the plane
to return to potable water and caged animals
I went for a walk to feel the textiles in the market.
While he wrote out the formula for the rise of activism,
I wrapped myself in shawls, smelled garlic, tasted achiote.
I returned to the ceiling fan and my lover still dripping
on the stone tiles, his beard entirely shaved away,
his face preacher slick, clean, smelling of bureaucracy.
He had mapped out guerrillas, revolutionaries,
subcomandantes.
I touched his face, and he drew back.

It's over he said almost clinically, almost cheerfully.
It was time for us to move on, don't you think, cheerio?

III
Red

Our Bedclothes

No one wears a negligee any more.
No one wears corsets, garters, five inch heels.
No one waxes off their eyebrows, pencils them back in.
Ah the Shirleys dreaming, poufing their hair
rouging their cheeks, powdering their faces.
We are so modern and sure of ourselves.
No man would marry us even if we wanted
to ball and chain him and we don't.
We wear jocky underwear and our fathers' wife-beaters.
If someone whistles, we'll sue him for harassment
where he stands. We're alone with our empty ovens
and our one glass of wine. We've got it all.
If I ate a potato for supper tonight,
skins and all, what's it to you?
I climb the stairs. Up there is a skylight,
a round porthole you can see clouds or smog,
smog though, mostly.

Fishers of Men

The invitation to fish for men
came as no surprise
to the fishers of Galilee.
The country was full of Messiahs.

The idea of following the Grateful Dead
or the Doors was certainly better
than cutting off heads, tails, fins.
The job stank; flies followed them.

Simon and Andrew left their nets
to found a church that would kill
countless in the Crusades,
millions in the Inquisition.

When Jesus died, they didn't want to stop
the honey days of walking and women,
fresh figs on the road
to return to fishing, tax collecting.

Like the band of a dead rock star,
they began to tell stories.
Elvis is alive. Jim Morrison is alive.
I saw him on the road to Emmaeus.

The death.
The myth.
The religion.
The killing for the religion.

The fishers said we're not going back to work.
Other people will send us money.
Tell a story, make it a good story,
and the TV evangelists said, Amen.

We read myths to children before they sleep
so they will grow up to be heroes.
Religion to grown ups so we can know who to kill
or who God will kill when he gets around to it.

Reasons to Undress a Woman Quickly

Hurry, his hands say, rapido,
although there is no rush.
Although she is not going anywhere.
But still he must move quickly
breaking a button stressing the fabric
until her spine lays bare
in the stretched open light
coming in past the windowsill.

He feels thirsty suddenly.
A bare table with one metal cup
full of water in arm's reach.
But he can't turn away
from the task at hand because
of the insufferable nights
when he could not trust
his idiot voice to speak again.

When he had said the right words
and under his mother's
shingled patio gotten so far,
been so bold in the streetlight.
Madre, Dios, he'd muttered,
hand moving past stockings.
And now he can't let it stop
because on so many shingled evenings

deep quiet along the streets
the folks already passed out
he'd moved wrong or spoken some word
or breathed, Dios,
even his breath could be a curse.
And her mind would be off and running
the disconnect switch he'd been playing with
all evening miles away.

Her little voice chattering about the prom
or her mother or her girlfriend's blouse
or anything and damn, damn, damn.
He hurries through the undressing now.
He cannot take a chance.
He prays while he loosens her hair
He hurries to make up for the nights
when finally

with the streetlights
he'd been safely alone,
kissing his hands in the dark
thinking what a waste,
what a terrible waste
but good practice I guess.

Cities

When she lived in New York
she was full of plans
for Los Angeles where
she would be palm happy
and sun licked
but after two years
of running after money
on Los Angeles freeways
she was frail as a wraith
and ready to scream so she
moved to Athens to be a waitress
write poetry naked
on the beaches
Athens gave out
when she couldn't find work
and then Rome Paris London
Cairo was a disaster
She seemed to invite
a steady stream of offers
from seedy pimps
She would dream of the lucky
people in the next city
the one where she wasn't living
she'd get out the crumpled world map
start saving for the next move
pack up whatever fit
in her rucksack
In Hong Kong she found a job
teaching Spanish
which led to flute lessons
What caused her to stop
eventually
in San Francisco
with a Chinese immigrant
was the idea of clean laundry

every day
It was simple
He would wash her dresses
He would hand them back to her
perfect.

Trains

My aunt gave me Coronas which I nearly drank,
swallowing gold at 10:30 in the morning.
But the train smelled of coffee and little people
and the Coronas seemed out of place.
Los Angeles was aglow with smog,
the bougainvilleas drunk with the kind of happiness
that happens when you don't realize you could be anywhere else.
The palm trees heavy with dreams of palm trees someplace else
where there's a water table running over.
When I'm not on the train, I dream of other people
train dancing into New York. Like a Morrison novel
where everything smells like fried food and happiness.
Somebody's life in motion, while mine just hangs there
like dew on a spiderweb.
When I'm on the train, you're some other place.
I'm dreaming of hands happening to somebody else
Hands and eyes, hair and fingers.
Sweat maybe.
Kisses even.

Trapping Rats and Other Problems

Living with others leads to
the trapping of rats and other problems.
Every house with others is a mad house.
Living alone, no one sees you lick
your soup bowl, then ice cream eat and lick.

No one knows you eat boiled onions and eggs
at three a.m. while ironing.
No one knows what you do with scallions.
If beer is cheaper, all the better
champagne is foolish if you are alone.

There is no reason to leave the house
turn off the television. Bathing is optional.
Cleaning house unnecessary. Any food that requires
pounding, grinding, sauteing, broiling,
toasting, frying, a waste of effort.

You're better off sleeping under the bed or in a chair.
Forget personal hygiene and the telephone.
Just crouch gnome like on the green carpet with brown stains
or the brown carpet with green stains by the television,
swimming in your own private glass blue world.

Eat Salisbury steak from the microwave
Watch reruns. Your tv days will lose
those jerky disconnected moments when
you know what time it is, will connect filament
like to each other.

Don't scream
People might hear you.
You don't want them to come in, do you?
You don't want them to think you're crazy,
Do you?

Giraffe Tongues and Cherries

The woman's feet are heavy, shapeless.
She wears thongs with socks, a coarse sweater.
She keeps hitching her girdle.
I see she isn't wearing a bra.
She says domestic violence
is a terrible thing and keeps her
from having a decent home life.
She says she can't imagine
what she'd do without her television
and a whole lot of prayer.

Because her husband wasn't always like that.
They used to go to the zoo to watch the giraffes
lick each other slowly with long blue tongues.
They laughed easily when those long necks
stretched for leaves almost out of reach.
But after the earthquake
they started to notice cracks in the walks
and some of their fence fell down.
The fierce gods were after them.
Pretty soon it wasn't just the two of them.

The neighborhood was trooping through their house
like it was one vast garage.
A public garage is not a home; it's a filthy place
with all kinds of people coming and going,
money changing hands. Most of the time
you can't tell who works there,
fans running, the radio jarring and thumping.
You can't remember what you came for .
Somebody's yelling that they got a raw deal
and maybe it's you; maybe it's everybody.

She says I went to the zoo alone last week.
The leaves were out of reach.
The giraffes were eating hay.
I think it was mouldy.
they looked bored, caged, no room to run.
I doubt they remember life before the cage.
I doubt they would know what to do with space.
On the bus home, someone gave me a basket of cherries.
I kept staring at in my lap,
all those little unrecognizable faces.

The Dream You Couldn't Leap Across

Dreams are huge expanses we fall across
to become other people. We find our way
through tangled leaf shaped
light patterns shifting across the driveway.

I had a husband once, then we branched out
to become other foliage.
Sometimes I'd hear the curtains singing.
I'd walk over to a bowl of onions and oranges.

The phone would begin ringing.
When I was a wife, the food turned out wrong.
He'd want something Midwestern the night
I was stirring up something ethnic.

The kitchen was scallions and curry,
the sink full of red cabbages and blue dishes.
Half the time the potatoes were boiling over.
The other half, sticking to the bottom of the pan.

Then I'd notice fig leaves growing out of the rusting fence
like ears listening to everything we'd say,
and morning glories thrusting their faces
from the spokes of bicycle wheels.

Nothing got repaired at our house. The garbage disposal stank.
There were fines for waste oil improperly disposed of.
I hid the blood, the ashes, the fish guts, the old papers,
the crumpled letters and diaries.

In the end, there was the dream we couldn't leap across.
The moment of waking was always crouched in long shadows.
Finally, there wasn't enough sleep time. There was too much
light washing in around us, unravelling us, whispering,

what are you doing?
what are you doing?

What is Left

for Christie

Since they had barely begun marriage
they had plenty of dishes
a bed which lacked pillows
the kind you lean against to read
but had several army blankets
donated by the groom's aunt
who said California is not necessarily warm
They had a tray of baklava
left over from the reception
so they wouldn't go hungry

On the fourth day of marriage
she was grading papers
he was shaving over the sink
humming "Appalachian Spring" for the third time
She climbed back over the anticipation
the moment when she touched the dress to her cheek
the moment of longing and fatigue
when she saw the rings side by side
the liquid stillness in the room
when he kissed her mouth like taking an apple

She makes onion soup
the room crowded with people's faces
asking her what's left now? what will happen
to the days that stretch out like blankets
you can weave one after another
the colors and texture all your choice
Only I'm not a weaver
Nobody in my tribe taught weaving
It was done at night while I was sleeping
or they stopped weaving when I came in the room

He enters smelling of soap,
closes his hands
over hers and the soup spoon
Together their hands move the onions
What are we making? he asks

Next to the Freeways

You see the outside of tires
spinning too fast out of control
then the skin comes off
hits the guard rail
bounces down the center divider
lands on the freeway hits a car

arcs and rocks tire crazy
to the side of the freeway
next to a dead animal
wet fur species
you cannot tell if it is a dog
a coyote or a cat at this stage

The freeway rushes along
a shiny trail of cars
beside tire rims and skins
hearts and flesh
dead bodies of animals wild and domestic
Animals thrown out of cars

what you see is what we don't want
we wish it would vanish
on contact with earth
we have no more use for these bodies
what are they but the remains
of what should never have been

the flesh by the freeways
reminds us of our own flesh
skin of an apple skin of a dog
skin like your skin
the refuse is heaped up
carted away

When the Aswan Dam was built
huge earth movers dug into the
soil to tear it back
for all that concrete
all those layers of skin
lost somewhere

North America explored by skin traders
Trading for silver fox rabbit wolf
The sun stares into skins by the freeway
Cars travel to distant planets carrying fur traders
skin travellers willing to bargain flesh
and if not to discard it in orbit.

Missing the Crow

When she enters the classroom,
the teacher stops to consider the slack face
bruised jaw recently bloodied mouth
nods briefly and continues stretching out
lines of poetry on the board
like a net for catching the falling

But not for Aliya
Aliya's hands are scorched
on the backs of the knuckles
her eyebrows singed and when the teacher
kneels beside her to ask a question
the eyes settle on another student's blouse

There are bars on the window
she says there is no light
I told my husband he was evil
He washed out my mouth
with soap for lying
Said I did this to myself

He went outside to wash his car
He uses Turtle Wax
He asked me to make him some pork ribs
He likes them very well done
I had to go to the hospital
to get my ribs taped first

I didn't get to dinner until late
so I understand
why he brought in Merilee
to suck him off
I couldn't have done it
my mouth such a mess

There's a crow in the tree by my apartment
crows are vicious dirty loud
I'm going to miss that crow
when you take me someplace Teacher
what's it going to be?
some room where light moves differently?

Not Needing the Sun

When love shivered and walked away
on tiny cold feet,
you held the pieces . . .

the rug on the floor
the way the light
holds back darkness
from slipping
in from the hallway
and being all around one
in the bed
the way any noise
keeps one from having
to put one thought against another

to put a memory together
piece by shining piece
the movement of eyes
the crook of a neck
the hooking of fingers over a belt
the flick flick of the candle
the way the light failed
to support the image
of happiness in the face
looking into yours

the way that unhappiness
spilled over to you
the way it spilled everywhere
smudged the tablecloth
the milk you were drinking turned sour
the rice cold
and you felt tired
very soon after you got
out of bed
because being awake was useless

the way the tiger lilies in the front walk
looked distorted too orange
the stamens too obvious
the way one morning
you wake envious of how others
feel spongy and glad
for the coming day
ready to soak it all in
and you feel that way
yourself a little

as if you'd somehow
been wounded
but had emerged from
the trauma ward
into the light sunny air
unscathed
the wounds very fresh and visible
but somehow not so important
now that you're outside
and the breeze is blowing

you could stop and look back
but you don't
you take a breath
testing the air for particles
it is clean and you swear
the sheer weight of the sky seems lighter
perhaps you will reach into the next day
find space for your hands and feet
the florescent weight of your days
has shifted

and the sun inside you feels obvious
and for a moment you are aware
of your own radiance

She Told me of Hitting Her She Would Cure Him

Far away light coming up to her eyelids
whispering it's daytime
She pulls up slowly still bandaged,
starts remembering heel boot fist
the heavy slap
the high whine of her engine
her daughter saying
Come on the car's started
the light pattering of feet
how she'd finally said
You go
There is something I have to finish here
Her wrists ache
It is very cold
Far away a dead flapping
wet sheets or wings
The light is very far off becoming closer now
She was going to help him become a better man
If she hadn't been so tired all the time
And if the church hadn't been such a gossip place
and If
The clouds are all around her now
She smiles
The light is very close
The experience begins to rotate
She hears large white wings beating
sees herself drifting into the sun
falling down a water shaft into the ocean
becoming a cube of green silence
all possible
she thinks
Everything or nothing

Rinsing Cherries

Rinsing cherries she comes upon
a black spider who raises hairy legs
with an economy of movement
lifts herself away
from water and fruit
to the rim of the bowl
the lip of the sink
the faucet
the wall

The woman has been at work all day
has spoken only briefly
with her husband
her briefcase leans
against the door
she tastes one
of the rinsed cherries
Without a career
she could have tasted these cherries

the spider has made definite progress
she has attained the windowsill

You Never Married the Pope

She had poems tacked to apartment walls.
She had scrambled eggs in the pan,
carrot juice to wash them down.

She had willow sticks in the corner
cotton attached to the walls and ceiling
so the willow would think it was clouds.

She had glued stars between the clouds.
She slept on the living room floor
failed to comb her hair most days.

She was not the kind of woman
to whom you could tell secrets
so when you took her to yourself

pressing your fingers between shoulder blades
to massage out all grief
you knew what you were doing.

Don't tell me now you didn't.
You knew you hadn't married the pope.
You should have expected insanity shards for breakfast.

You should have expected that glass shoe
full of cement ready mix.
It meant something to you, didn't it?

Here's to new myths, she said, using
her ex-husband's antlers to imprison your underwear.
New symbols she said.

You say now that you got lost somewhere,
a vast mine field is what she was. You're still reeling
from finding her bra on your windshield.

What was that supposed to mean?
See the world through her breasts?
But the language of clothing is perhaps the simplest.

Lift her shirt.
Count her ribs.
Undergarments and will are arranged separately.

There's Nothing to Talk About in this Poem

Nothing interests me I guess
at least nothing but nails
and wet ferns and clouds
and fire also acorns
stew especially corn husk stew
which I've heard about but never eaten
and why women steal
other women's children
and turtles what their plans are
and the ears of cows are truly amazing
but god doesn't interest me very much
or self sacrifice or patriots or joy
but I would like to talk about
the mud flaps on trucks
and steers who are sent to market too early
but really there's precious little we could
talk about when it comes to morals
or ethics or human nature
unless you're really thinking about
pomegranates whiskey or staring eyes

IV
Green

Praying Mantises and Missiles

You have an idea.
You're going to change the world.
Take that same idea.
Let it stand up.
Let it walk backward.
Let it change you.
Big world full of people, pine cones,
pizza, peacekeeping missiles,
praying mantises eating their spouses,
pedophiles, preachers, pick-up sticks.
When the whole world envelops you,
close your eyes,
lie down where your whole body
touches the soil,
feel the chicken,
feel the egg.
feel stuff growing,
your hair, the soil,
trees could grow there
you could become a tree
any day now.

I Give You My Hand

Stick your hand into mine,
and you'll find a woman's hand
under all that fur.

What you think next is up to you.
For some, it's a woman's grasping hand
For some, a woman's needy hand.

You hold my hand,
feel your own hand shining
back into your palm.

The voices travelling up your arm
are your voices. Once a man held my hand
said, this hand wants to be in my trousers.

I stopped in the white light spilling
in around us, surprised that his hands
wanted to touch him, and that he would tell me.

My hand in your hand is only half human
is partly beast
rock and soil.

Some of you won't feel that at all
or you won't feel the human part
just the animal skin, fur, feathers.

I could let my hands touch the crowd in you
make you solitary until you felt
your own tree roots

light and landscape
your blood and your chlorophyll
your feet, claws, hooves, branches.

I could do this but the ocean
is too far back
the surface so much easier

the light too bright
when it enters the body
through photosynthesis.

The hand has fingernails
like turtle shells or talons
Take all this into account I say.

I take your hand. You take mine.
Hands hold weapons. Hands hold stories.
Hands hold other hands.

The Way I Learned to Write

There were words I had to leave behind,
moonlight, backward ponies.
Leaving flowers out seemed safest.
Trying for something surreal,
A trouble free rise of smoke and lavender.

No not lavender. Any shade
of purple is best left alone.
Perhaps a jaundiced smoke
rising in my poetry
would be best, although I like violet haze.

Many a summer morning,
while other folks are
eating bagels, lox,
cinnamon rolls,
I rummage through old cider houses,

find words like obdurate,
bipolar, manic, cold heeled.
But writing about love, well,
not even searches to junkyards
as far away as Peking

turn up the slightest unused vowel.
So, I make words up, create my own language.
You Chinese me in the roofy mornings.
You Japanese my legs in the spidery evenings.
Our children are the leggy offspring

of centipede afternoons. Our bedroom
is the Acropolis. You temple me backward.
I could bless you all the way to shadowland.
If we were not already steepled there,
our undergarments ruffianed off onto chairs.

You catapulted silence,
dogkissed, catlicked my paws
held my squeaks and rattles.
Where the rest had said, What's this?
You said, it's mine.

Witchy Hands

All night I couldn't sleep
I'd been dripping with the flu
spent the day writhing and cursing
the long spit of hair
slicked to the back of my neck

the frothy lump of covers
that seemed to move about the bed
the way language writhed
and made massive leaps
around the room eluding me

when someone entered the room
the words I wanted to say
were always hiding under the bed
finally I woke around dinnertime
into the cool slow spin of late afternoon

the yard a pool of orange light
the kids adrift in their hammocks
and skateboards time convoluted
I bathed and walked out feeling less solid
like a trespasser or a ghost

That night against
a sea of clean linens
my boat rocked endlessly
so I moved my witchy hands
to your side of the bed

at first my intentions
therapeutic and nurturing
but later just wondering
if you could hold the sheets
up like that all night and still sleep

Inventing Royalty in Bed

Last night, your face
pale gray, hollow ash in lamplight.
You smelled of tequila, olives, brine
after our day at the beach.
You bathed into a soapy swarm
of smells shuddering across your skin.
You walked toward the bed, fell on it
an avalanche on my senses.
You reached for me then
bruised and tired as we both were,
and you wanted your ocean again
your fishy world.

I tell myself you want me
because I'm too much for to miss,
my hips too glorious to pass up.
That it might be you,
excited by the slap of waves
or needing comfort
or just rowdy for loin food
isn't something I play with.
I choose clouds to sit on
that make me feel royal
because royalty is real,
not something you imagine or invent.

You Do Frighten Me

there's a blankness before i knew you or of you
or of the possibility of you
a blankness arched and hanging
like fog circling
i remember figures darting in and out of the life
that was mine
nobody stayed long
mostly my space was empty of possibilities

the stars had too many spaces between them
i liked the Milky Way best
the stars ran together there
like light might continue
from one star to the next
constellations dot to dot happiness
i could not figure out where number one was
so i could not fill in the lines

i found you lapping water with your cupped hands
you gave me evaporating mist off a lake
you father mother holiness
you fed me berries in a long path
away from darkness i felt my tongue
too much dependent on drops of water
from your hands
water gushing from the rock

i decided over and over to walk away
because loneliness
was better than wondering
when I'd be lonely
you splash out on the sheets
you pull me down the thin line of your tongue
oh please i say
being alone is as familiar as skin

i have no family
no one has ever
held my breath
like marigold seeds
planted them in the windowsill
like orange dreams
grow for me
you'll say

pour me wine i say
i must be sleeping
i must be dreaming
this is something like happiness
let me go back to dreams
and you'll say
i do don't i?
I do frighten you

and you'll smile
you hold my loneliness
taste it like fear
a safety blanket
i think about dissolving
you say hold on to it
if its worth something to you
you do whatever you want

The Edges of Elbow Sleep

What he says when he feels her
sliding out of bed is nothing.
He reclaims sleep and his own side of the bed
where her elbows have been jutting all night.

In a nightmare, her fist darts across
smacks his thick shoulder bounces off.
He moans, wakes, reaches for matches,
lights the blue candle by the bedside.

She dreams. He blows out the candle,
rubs his shoulder, curves himself to her body.
Now as he feels her rising
to take in the night air

with the blessing of thoughts
that rise from the floor
of the earth most nights
to settle in the ankles of palm trees,

he pulls blankets around his head
dissolving back into the loose remains of sleep.
In sleep, legs and arms form shells
to their twinned eyes glowing into each other

like two sides of a clam shell
pearly and so close as to be inseparable.
In this swiftly moving place where he sleeps
there is no cool rush of air

between his legs and shoulder blades
as she rises notebook in hand
into the morning and her own work.
There is no he no she

only an opening and shutting
auricle and ventricle, left, right,
the pauses, the breaths one takes
between yes and yes.

Undressing Kathy

"I wish you to undress,"
and she turns toward the mirror
repeats again,
her imagined lover's words.
"I wish you to undress,
show a little wrist or something."
She does not want to take off clothes
for anyone, but to open her wardrobe of secrets.

Walking to school at thirteen,
I saw my first naked man
bathing in an outdoor shower,
the mountain behind him ripe and green.
The man's skin was brown, hair on his body
amazing hair. His mouth open
taking in water and air
The man saw me and waved. I ran then.

I want to tell someone
about the trees.
My friends and I collected fungi,
slices of tree trunk.
They wrote "Jenny loves John,"
"April loves Dennis,"
drew heart shapes sometimes
for the word "love."

I took my fungi, large white hands,
buried them. My tree slabs
I kissed, held to my heart
and returned to earth.
It is not possible for this
to be mine, I thought,
though we had wooden chairs.
I couldn't separate slab from tree.

Oh, I'd tell you,
if you asked me to undress.
I dived down through brackish water
past sleeping water lilies and frogs
rose otter like for breath
swimming downstream to the dam
rising into the abandoned beaver's house.
I pulled myself up, out of water

These are gifts I would give you
if you asked me to undress.
The undressing would go on for years
would go on forever.

Holiness is . . .

A woman asks why not?
leans to her friend
across the man's lap
tastes her friend's mouth
soft petal delicate
Both women moan

the man between them
his mind and body
rush and whisper
wrists ankles legs shoulders
lips tongues
Perhaps confusion is in order

perhaps monogamy
so unnatural to the species
so necessary in a deadly world
insists on its own expansion
Woman to woman eye to eye
breast to breast thigh to thigh

Perhaps all it takes
is a woman to say why not?
Perhaps all it takes is a man
to say nothing
to remember tongues
are for everything but speech

The language we ask
is not spoken
It tilts backward
into the night primal feverish
Be part of candlelight
Let us own you.

Marsupial Love

Though I could barely clothespin my life to the line,
you kept practicing Latin in the stairway.
I had to go around you every time I climbed up and down.

When we met, I'd smoothed silks past my hips,
hoping my limber torso would invite you inside.
I'm a figure skater, each 8 I loop, creates

two places for you to jump,
the whole or the smaller whole.
But the silks gave way to wools,

the wools to dark corduroys,
restless polyester, faded cottons.
Until we have this--the smell of sesame oil.

I'll cook pasta, toss with oil, onions, garlic.
We'll eat late in the heavy light of the broken candle
while the cat meows on the steps.

We'll pick at the stained tablecloth
the shards of pottery left
from your last creative surge.

I'll feel the lump in my throat
as the circle closes.
Pretty soon we're not figure skating at all,

just marching in these tiny circles
that face into each other,
go nowhere at all.

Wooden Salt Shaker

He comes to the woman
clearly in the whole light of day
hands her a plate of fish, cucumbers, melons,
a wooden salt shaker.
They sit together on the floor
eating with their hands.
The cucumbers sting his fingers.
They have been rubbed in vinegar.
It gives him pleasure
to serve her this way,
and even to eat the fish
which he has never developed a taste for.
But the woman's pleasure is in seeing
him mouth to fish, just so,
her own private worship
from his mouth and fingers.
He moves to lick his fingers
and then she,
knowing that his tongue on his fingers
is her own imagination
kneels across the fish,
takes his fingers in her own mouth.
In another century
her desires might be considered impure.
But he, savage being that he is,
can carry her weight
up great flights of stairs
century after century.
When the fish scales slide
to the ground
he carries her to the little fountain,
holds her while she washes her face and hands
finally submerging her head and throat in liquid.
The fish had at first seemed some terrible dream
whitening his landscape,

but now with the cucumbers and melons
and her ready mouth,
he can bear it.

Ah, he laughs into the sun, all his teeth gleaming,
he can bear it.

Tuesdays

Today is a Tuesday, one of many.
He has a girl he loves every Tuesday,
her day off. He burns
at the fine fire of her conscience,

tells her they'll be married
someday. He has a wife,
Doreen, a freckle-faced fat thing
who harbors resentment that during her Tuesday

at her mother's, he insists on going to the movies.
Rose petals he picks up in the neighbor's yard
end up at Tuesday's feet and
sprinkled through the sheets.

Of course they must make love,
since he sees her only once a week.
Doreen requires sex after seeing her mother.
He feels like an ox on Tuesday, powerful and massive.

He tells this to Tuesday
and to Doreen.
Doreen tells him he is an ox
a brute master of the air and his rightful bed.

But Tuesday, who knows oxen
are slow moving, dim witted,
and castrated at birth,
follows him home instead of playing her dulcimer,

climbs the wall, watches him mounting his wife,
leaves rose petals on his doorstep,
takes the train to cornfields, steers and heifers
watches the city disappear in rain.

Thinks briefly of how tenderly
he rose in her fingers
while the remains of their breakfast,
eggs and potatoes

cooled on the wooden table
with the tattered tablecloth.

Reasons Why He Hurt You

He was in your house.
He was in your bed.
He was in your body.

He was in your dreams.
He was in your shadow.
He was in the clubhouse of your mind.

Scissors to dreams
Scissors to shadows.
Leave dream shards, shadow fragments.

You said come here.
You said look at this map
Here's where the Tiber meets the Euphrates.

He said, Here's the Valley of the Kings
one sarcophagus after another.
My specialty he said, all teeth.

You have to explore the same part of the map.
Yes, you say, I know, one river at a time.
And now, how do I get this tomb out of my belly?

Breakfast

1.

Lox, sliced tomatoes, red onions, cream cheese.
Clouds moving. Summer breaking.
I am leaving you.

2.

Bagels, fresh squeezed orange juice.
Not enough roof over the house. Rain coming in.
Why? I have a right to know.

3.

Hard boiled eggs, salt and pepper.
Fence needs repair. Dog getting out.
You have no rights, Nobody has any rights.
Nothing I'm ready to talk about.

4.

Lettuce, raspberries, goat cheese, cilantro.
Mail doesn't arrive any more.
But if you have to know.
If you have to carry around something as an explanation.
I don't love you any more.

Bed Vision

The man in the orange hat is thinking about his wife last night,
how she advanced on him in the twilight of their bedroom
her green bathrobe askew, pale face, slanted view of her
frontal nudity through the string only half tied.
She had a way of arranging herself on the bed beside him
either concealing or revealing.
Her choice was his cue of the night's activities.
It's all up to Janet, he thinks. It's decided in the shower.
Nothing I do afterward makes much difference.
He'd gotten home early yesterday to plant red geraniums
in the window box, and that did it.
But usually the path to revealing thighs beside him in bed
was much more complicated, fraught with pitfalls.
Once she'd gotten turned off when he mentioned "corn"
and "celery" in the same sentence
as she had mentioned to him previously not to talk about either.
They reminded her of her father.
There is a list with women his friend Eduardo tells him
of things you can and cannot do.
They make up this shitty list as they go along
and they change it every day.
Men are in ready mode except when asleep
But for women, there is a long series
of treacherous waters, dams to portage over
barely navigable rivers, waterfalls to climb bareheaded.
Eduardo has a woman named Jeanine.
He says talking with Jeanine
is like driving toward a cliff blindfolded.
You know there's an edge you won't feel until you go over.
They know they're making us criminally insane
but they keep going, Eduardo says.
But the man in the orange hat is smiling in the face of the sun.
Thinking how after childbirth, she held the baby and said
she only half remembered the pain now.

He, remembering her driving force last night,
fingernails, dizzy heat,
is pretty sure he understands how that vivid pain
becomes confused and blotted with suffused warmth
abated longing.

Across the Street

At night, after television,
my husband and I sit smoking, staring out.
We watch the lights go out in the bedroom
across the street, the flare of candles.
Then it's shadow puppet time.
We watch our neighbors moving in the dark,
their figures black on the curtains,
the woman's hair, a flying tangle against the light.
On television sitcoms, the hair is usually lit
from behind and appears to glow.
I have not touched my husband for years except by accident.
We're a decent American couple.
We don't actually garden.
We do a lot of yard work.
We attend air shows.
On weekends, I clean floors.
We used to attend church.
Now we watch TV evangelists.
I like to smoke and watch them.
The only problem I have is across the street.
If they weren't doing that,
we wouldn't be watching.
If we weren't watching,
we wouldn't be thinking.
If we weren't thinking,
we wouldn't be dreaming.
If we weren't dreaming,
I'd be safe.
Watching sitcoms,
going to sleep
without thoughts rushing through me
like fluid, like restless electricity
from my breasts to my legs, to my fingers,
down, down, stop me, Lord.
I'm a good woman.

I pray for strength.
I can't keep praying
with those shadows twisting.
I try to sing, buy my husband stops me.
We struggle with our faith all night
We'll have to sleep today
if we're going to stay up tonight
to pray for that couple across the street.

The Emperor's New Clothes

Gertrude Stein.
We could end there.
But we won't.
Because we want to make meaning.
Of something.
to say something.
Of value.
In order that.
It's absolutely.
The professor said.
Wiggling his ears.
In a satisfied way.
And the students all said, Amen.
That's the way with critical acclaim.
Absolutely.
There are rooms.
There are builders.
There is a clock.
There is a cake.
There is a rope.
There is a sounding to depths.
But when she dies, what then?
Who knew what it all meant?
And when all the modernists are dead?
The critics will babble and frenzy
forever to find the nouns she never wrote
between the crowded verbs and adverbs.

Tundra Races

Poetry is a place
where, when madness occurs
nobody notices;

or if they do
it's called genius.
It's one of the reasons

I'm so comfortable with poetry.
Other art forms require sanity,
at least in short bursts.

Painting allows for certain
lapses, but only poetry
can be wildly

careening from its kinetic purpose
gyrating in its own orbit
yet produce awe

in critics willing to stare
at the naked poet
bloody cold on the tundra

call to each other
from one borough to the next
how brilliant

the texture
the threads of meaning
the overall pattern of color and light.

The poet knows;
Ah, he or she knows.
Bloody cold, we whisper.

There are two themes in all of Kate Gale's poetry that weave and struggle and weave together again like two line of a fugue: A life filled with oppression from an early age (sexual, religious) and the wonder that the poet discovers just outside it. What finally rises through the suffering is a celebratory love of life and a surprising compassion. I believe these new poems to be her best yet.

— Doug Anderson,
author of *The Moon Reflected Fire*